FERRIES OF
SCOTLAND

John Hendy

VOLUME 2

ISBN 1 871947 48 0
PO Box 9, Narberth, Pembrokeshire SA68 0YT

D1426227

Foreword by Lord Gordon of Strathblane
Chairman of the Scottish Tourist Board

In these days of feverishly fast-moving lifestyles, Scotland's uncrowded natural environment, dramatic scenery and romantic, turbulent history are powerful magnets for a tourism market that last year attracted over 13 million visitors to our shores and generated £2.655 billion of expenditure. Our wild and spectacular landscapes, feisty and friendly people and distinctive culture enable us to compete in a global marketplace where every year visitors are presented with more opportunities to spend their tourism £s than ever before.

Scotland's ferry services play a crucial role in the tourism industry. Thanks to private and public sector ferry companies, essential transport is provided to some of Scotland's most stunning scenery and popular tourism destinations. By the same token, it is largely revenue generated from the tourism season that enables ferry companies to service island populations throughout the year.

For our visitors, ferries are not simply a method of getting from A to B. The ferry crossing forms an integral part of the holiday experience, adding a sense of adventure. My regular visits to Iona, crossing first to Mull and then from there to Iona, gives me the sense that I am distancing myself ever further from the stresses and strains of every day living. At sea, the magic of the islands and their rich historical legacy are brought vividly to life. Ferry travel also provides a spectacular perspective on one of the longest, most unspoilt and wildlife-rich coastlines in Europe. Island visitors arriving by sea can anticipate the opportunity to spot seals, whales, dolphins, porpoise and sea-birds, the memory of which will stay with them long after their feet touch dry land.

Improving and developing transport links throughout the Scottish Isles is vital in order for Scotland to maintain and improve her reputation as both a quality and accessible destination. The service between Ullapool and Stornoway has recently been reduced to under three hours which is the kind of good news that will keep our tourism industry buoyant. I look forward to seeing further developments within the ferry industry that improve the quality of the services we provide for our visitors and moves that support our drive to extend the season beyond the summer months. I am delighted Caledonian MacBrayne and Stena are participating in our 1998 Autumn Gold Marketing campaign.

Introduction

It is now some six years since the first edition of this book appeared and the opportunity has been taken to reprint the title offering a completely new set of photographs for the followers of the Scottish ferry scene. We have increased the size of the book and have also excluded the larger cross-Channel vessels operating from Stranraer and Cairnryan as these are dealt with in the companion volume, "Ferries of the Irish Sea."

This latest publication in no way includes all present day ships but it attempts to portray a broad sample of the rich variety of ferries which both have served and which continue to operate from, in and around Scotland. While some of the older vessels as seen within these pages never earned the title 'ferry' the expression is used in its widest possible sense so as to include some of the classic coastal ships of the past.

As ever, my grateful thanks must go to the photographers who have kindly answered my requests in **European Ferry Scene** and sent examples of their work for inclusion within these pages. Thanks are also due to Ian Hall who has kindly read and checked through the text and made helpful comments concerning it.

Whenever possible I have tried to include ships in a location rather than simply with a blank sea as a background as to many people it is the topography of the west coast, just as much as the vessels which ply to and from its small piers and harbours, which typifies the Scottish ferry scene.

I mentioned in the first edition (and its subsequent reprint) that reading these pages will be very much a second-best experience. No picture can adequately portray the magnificent panoramas and the clean, clear air of the highlands and islands but it is hoped that by looking at the photographs and reading their captions, the reader will be encouraged to visit these unique places and share the remarkable and rewarding experience which they offer.

John Hendy

The *Claymore* was built in 1978 for the Oban - Outer Isles service where she replaced the *Iona*. She soon proved to be too small and the new *Lord of the Isles* replaced her in 1989 after which time she was switched to the Kennacraig - Islay route. The summers of 1994-96 saw the ship tried on a new service linking Ardrossan and Douglas (Isle of Man) and in the following year she was sold to Sea Containers for service on the seasonal Campbeltown - Ballycastle (Antrim) crossing under the flag of the Argyll & Antrim Steam Packet Company (Lawrence Macduff)

The Caledonian Steam Packet Co's *Duchess of Argyll* was their first turbine steamer and entered service in 1906 on the Ardrossan - Arran route. Between the wars she served Arran (via the Kyles of Bute) and later Inveraray She was sold to the Admiralty for experimental purposes in 1952, her hull remaining intact until 1970 (A.M. Young)

The *Isle of Arran* was built for the Ardrossan - Brodick (Arran) service in 1984 and quickly became a victim of her own success, generating more traffic than she could comfortably handle. On the arrival of her successor, she was transferred to the Kennacraig - Islay service on which she is seen sporting the third and most recent style of hull paint application. (Lawrence Macduff)

Replacing the *Isle of Arran* came the *Caledonian Isles* in 1993. With her capacity for 1,000 passengers and 120 cars she was at that time the largest unit in the CalMac fleet. The peaks of Arran are snow-clad as she nears Ardrossan on Christmas Eve 1995. (Lawrence Macduff)

The *Caledonian Isles* approaches Brodick (Arran) in July 1996. This well-appointed vessel has been a great boon to the island's tourist industry and offers passengers all-round deck views. Ship owners are realising that their customers enjoy a forward view! (B.W.J. Shaw)

The *Pioneer* arriving at Brodick (Arran) on a sailing from Rothesay via Largs in July 1996. The ship was built in 1974 to operate between West Loch Tarbert and Port Ellen (Islay). Since 1989 she has been the spare vessel and began her summer Rothesay - Largs - Brodick services in 1995. (R. Stewart Cameron)

The last of the line. The preserved paddle steamer *Waverley* leaving Brodick (Arran) on a cruise from Ayr to Campbeltown in July 1996. The steamer was built in 1947 and, following her withdrawal from service, was sold to the Paddle Steamer Preservation Society for £1 in 1974. Since then she has circumnavigated Britain and has become something of an institution. (R. Stewart Cameron)

The Loch class vessel *Loch Ranza* entered service in 1987 on the seasonal 'back door' service linking Claonaig and Lochranza (Arran). Since 1992 she has mainly been associated with the Gigha service. (Brian Maxted)

The clouds are low over the hills of Arran as the Loch class ferry *Loch Tarbert* leaves Claonaig for Lochranza in July 1997. (David Robertson)

The *Isle of Cumbrae* of 1977 back on her original service linking Cumbrae Slip with Largs in September 1997. Since being replaced on the route by the larger Loch class vessels in 1986 she has served at Lochaline, Kyle of Lochalsh and Colintraive. (Iain McPherson)

The *Lord of the Isles* approaching Port Bannatyne (Bute) in July 1924. She was built for the Glasgow & Inveraray Steamboat Company in 1891 for the Glasgow - Inveraray service. Her ownership passed to Turbine Steamers Ltd. in 1912 for whom she operated around Bute and later to Lochgoilhead and Arrochar (Loch Long) before her eventual demise in 1928. (A.M. Young)

The Glasgow & South Western Railway's steamer *Mercury* near Rothesay (Bute) in June 1921. She was built in 1892 and was mainly used on the Kyles of Bute services. After an eventful war minesweeping (during which time she lost both her stern and later her bow) she returned to service and was finally withdrawn for breaking in 1933. (A.M. Young)

The LNER steamer *Kenilworth* leaving Rothesay (Bute) in August 1924. She was built in 1898 for the North British Steam Packet Co. and was broken up forty years later. (A.M. Young)

The CSP turbine steamer *Duchess of Hamilton* approaching Rothesay in 1968. Built as the Ayr excursion steamer in 1932, the ship enjoyed a successful 38 year career with the Caledonian Steam Packet Company. (A.M. Young)

MacBrayne's diesel electric vessel *Lochfyne* was built in 1931 for summer excursion services from Oban to Staffa and Iona and winter work as the Ardrishaig mail vessel. She later worked from Fort William and after the *Saint Columba* had been withdrawn in 1958 took over the summer Ardrishaig route. She is crossing Rothesay Bay in 1968. (A.M. Young)

The *Caledonia* entered service in 1934 and she is seen in Rothesay Bay during 1968, the year before she was withdrawn from service. She was built for the railway connected services from Greenock, Gourock and Wemyss Bay but when replaced by the ABC car ferries in 1954 she became the Ayr excursion steamer. Purchased by Bass Charrington's Brewery for static use on the Thames she was damaged by fire in 1980 after which she was broken up near Sittingbourne in Kent. Her engines have been preserved. (A.M. Young)

The Island class ferry *Bruernish* at Rothesay (Bute). After operating on the Tarbert - Portavadie link in 1997 she became a spare vessel in 1998. She has accommodation for 164 passengers or 50 passengers and 6 cars. (Brian Maxted)

Originally a side-loader used on the Skye ferry, the *Portree* (and sister *Broadford*) were moved to the newly acquired secondary Bute route in 1970. Converted to bow-loading they worked the Kyles of Bute crossing until replaced by larger tonnage in 1986. The *Portree* is seen at Rhubodach in 1985. (Iain R. Murray)

Sailing on a mirror-like Kyles of Bute the *Loch Riddon* nears Colintraive on the secondary Bute service from Rhubodach. In 1997 she was switched to the Largs - Cumbrae Slip route. (Lawrence Macduff)

The Loch class ferry *Loch Alainn* at Colintraive on her first ever spell on the secondary service to Bute in July 1997. Originally intended for the Sound of Mull service linking Lochaline and Fishnish (Mull), the vessel now appears to have found a home at Largs. (Iain McPherson)

One of the eight Island class ferries, the *Rhum* is seen arriving at Portavadie at the conclusion of the twenty minute crossing of Loch Fyne from Tarbert - the service which she inaugurated in 1994. She has recently been sold to Irish owners. (Brian Maxted)

The *Sound of Shuna* (ex. *Olandssund IV*) opened Western Ferries' Cowal link in June 1973. After a period as relief boat she may be switched to start a new service linking Cowal with Bute. (Brian Maxted)

Western Ferries' *Sound of Sleat* was built as the *De Hoorn* in 1961 to operate across the New Waterway near Rotterdam. She has operated on the company's Upper Firth link since 1988. (A.M. Young)

Western Ferries' *Sound of Sanda* at Hunter's Quay. Formerly the *G24* of Amsterdam City Council she was purchased by her Scottish owners in 1996. (Brian Maxted)

Western Ferries' *Sound of Scalpay* is the sister vessel of the *Sound of Sanda*. She was built for the Amsterdam City Council as the *G23* in 1961 and was purchased for use on the Upper Clyde in 1995. Capacity is for 220 passengers and 37 cars. (Lawrence Macduff)

The car ferry *Arran* (photographed in 1961) was the lead ship for three identical vessels built in 1953 for the Gourock - Dunoon, Wemyss Bay - Rothesay (Bute) and Fairlie - Brodick (Arran) routes. In her original state the *Arran* could hoist load 26 cars although later modifications increased this to 34. Sisters *Bute* and *Cowal* completed the ABC trio. (A.M. Young)

In 1953 the Caledonian Steam Packet Company ordered four iden
diesel powered ships to operate high frequency ferry services on the U
Clyde. The *Maid of Ashton* was followed by the *Maid of Argyll, Ma*
Skelmorlie and *Maid of Cumbrae*. After her withdrawal from servic
was decided to convert the *Maid of Cumbrae* to car ferry operation and
re-entered service from Gourock to Dunoon in May 1972. This was on
short term measure and with the entry into service of the *Juno* in Decen
1974 she was down-graded to spare vessel before being sold to Italy
years later. Accommodation was for only 15 cars which were mo
exposed to the elements. (A.M. Young)

Seen when new in 1970 the MacBrayne car ferry *Iona* on charter to the Caledonian Steam Packet Company (yellow funnel) and arriving at Dunoon from Gourock. The dummy funnel was removed early in 1975 when extra cabins were built on the upper deck for use on the Oban – Outer Isles service. The ship's twin exhausts were lengthened by 6 ft. at the same time. (A.M. Young)

Dressed overall at Gourock the *Juno* awaits the departure of her Sunday cruise to Tarbert (Loch Fyne) during August 1996. The Clyde Marine Motoring Company's *Kenilworth* lies ahead of her. (R. Stewart Cameron)

The *Saturn* is seen on service between Dunoon and Gourock. Built in 1978 as the last of the three Upper Clyde 'streakers', the ship was initially associated with the Wemyss Bay - Rothesay (Bute) link although her roster are today interwoven with those of her half-sisters *Jupiter* and *Juno*. (Lawrence Macduff)

The Clyde excursion steamer *Queen Mary II* is seen leaving Dunoon. Originally built for Williamson Buchanan Steamers in 1933 the vessel gained the suffix 'II' to make way for the Cunard liner of the same name. Withdrawn from service in 1977, the ship is now a floating restaurant up river from Waterloo Bridge in London. (A.M. Young)

The *Saturn* alongside at Tarbert (Loch Fyne) on one of her Sunday cruises during September 1994. At one time most villages on the Firth of Clyde boasted a pier at which steamers would call. With the growth of road transport, most of these have fallen into disuse. (Iain McPherson)

The first of the Clyde 'streakers' was the *Jupiter* which entered service on the Gourock - Dunoon route in March 1974. She is seen off the Renfrewshire port in March 1996. (Lawrence Macduff)

A powerful view of the *Juno* approaching Gourock from Dunoon in April 1995. She was built as the second of the Clyde 'streakers' entering service in December 1974. Capacity is for 531 passengers and 40 cars. (Iain R. Murray)

The Clyde Marine Motoring Company operate the *Kenilworth* on the Gourock - Kilcreggan - Helensburgh service. The former *Hotspur II* was built for the Hythe - Southampton ferry service in 1936 and was acquired by her present owners in 1978. (David Robertson)

The only three funnelled Clyde steamer this century was MacBrayne's *Saint Columba* which was built for Turbine Steamers Ltd as the *Queen Alexandra* in 1912. In 1935 she was sold to David MacBrayne Ltd., reconditioned and appeared with the third funnel before being placed on the Glasgow (Bridge Wharf) - Ardrishaig service where she replaced the famous paddle steamer *Columba*. She was withdrawn from service after her 1958 season. (A.M. Young)

The Caledonian Steam Packet Company's paddle steamer *Marchioness of Lorne* entered service on the Holy Loch run in 1935, a route on which she spent most of her career. She was broken up in 1955. (A.M. Young)

The David MacBrayne paddle steamer *Columba* dated from 1878 and became the most famous vessel of her type on the Clyde. She was used on the first stage of the Royal Route from Glasgow (Bridge Wharf) to Ardrishaig and was very much the society boat of her day. The vessel lasted until 1936 and is seen here off Gourock in June 1914. (A.M. Young)

The *Waverley* (left) and *Talisman* at the old LNER railhead of Craigendoran in 1949. The pier was closed to traffic in 1972. (A.M. Young)

The *Prince Edward* was built for services on Loch Lomond on which she first appeared in 1912. She continued in service after the advent of the *Maid of the Loch* but was broken up at Balloch in 1955. (A.M. Young)

Undergoing restoration at Balloch Pier is the paddle steamer *Maid of the Loch* of 1953. Out of service since August 1981 and today owned by the Loch Lomond Steamship Company, it is hoped to return the 45 year old vessel to service. (A.M. Young)

The David MacBrayne steamer *Pioneer* at her West Loch Tarbert berth in November 1923. She was built for the Islay service in 1905 but was replaced by the diesel vessel *Lochiel* in 1939. Taken over by the Admiralty during the Second World War, the *Pioneer* became a research ship and later a floating laboratory before being broken up in 1958. (A.M. Young)

MacBrayne's *Lochiel* of 1939 at the company's West Loch Tarbert pier loading for Islay. Withdrawn in 1970 she briefly saw service from Fleetwood to the Isle of Man before becoming a floating public house for Courage's Brewery in Bristol Docks where she was broken up in 1997. (A.M. Young)

Western Ferries (Argyll) Ltd. operated the small ferry *Sound of Gigha* on the 5 minute crossing between Port Askaig (Islay) and Feolin (Jura) from 1969-98. The vessel was built three years earlier as the *Isle of Gigha* to serve in a diesel 'puffer' role. She was replaced by a new vessel and operator in 1998. (Matthew Punter)

The *Isle of Arran* and *Sound of Gigha* meet in the Sound of Islay off Port Askaig (Islay) during July 1997. (Matthew Punter)

Every road leads to a ferry crossing! The *Isle of Arran* is berthed bow-in at Kennacraig. (Brian Maxted)

The Argyll & Bute Council operate the 5 car, 40 passenger ferry *Balnahua* on the service linking Seil and Luing
She was built at Campbeltown in 1973. (Brian Maxted)

The *Loch Buie* was was purpose-built for the Iona service and commenced operations in June 1992. Although one of the Loch class of ferry, she boasts capacity for 250 passengers but only 9 cars. Iona Abbey can be seen in the distance as the vessel nears Fionnphort (Mull) in July 1995. (Lawrence Macduff)

The *Arran* arriving at Oban during a spell on the Craignure (Mull) operation. The ship was converted to stern loading for the Islay link in 1973 at which time she lost her after superstructure. She was replaced by the *Pioneer* a year later and after a period in reserve, was eventually sold for static use in Dublin. (A.M. Young)

The *Clansman* as she appeared at Oban in July 1975 when working the Craignure (Mull) car ferry. The vessel was the second of three identical ferries built for MacBrayne's West Highland services.She entered service on the Mallaig - Armadale (Skye) route in 1964 and in 1973 was stretched and converted to drive-through operations for the Ullapool - Stornoway (Lewis) link. Replaced there by the *Suilven* in 1974, the *Clansman* was then switched to the Ardrossan - Brodick (Arran) route before being sold to Torbay Seaways in 1984 and then Maltese owners in the following year. (A.M. Young)

The Oban - Craignure (Mull) vessel *Isle of Mull* arriving at Colonsay on one of her thrice weekly visits. Traffic on the primary Mull service has risen to such an extent that there are plans to drop the loss-making Colonsay calls and link the island once more with a regular service from Kennacraig - a longer and less convenient crossing. (Brian Maxted)

The *Isle of Mull* has served the Oban - Craignure (Mull) route since her introduction in 1988. Serious deadweight problems saw an extra 20 ft. added to her hull in the following winter. Her capacity is for 1,000 passengers and 0 cars. She is seen arriving in Oban Bay with the Firth of Lorn beyond the island of Kerrera. (Iain McPherson)

The Outer Isles car ferry *Lord of the Isles* entered service in 1989 but her capacity for just 506 passengers and 6 cars was soon found wanting. With the arrival of the new *Clansman*, the ship was transferred to the Mallaig tation. (A.M. Young)

The *Rosehaugh* is operated by the Highland Council who maintain the link between Corran and Ardgour across Loch Linnhe. Originally built for the service between Inverness and the Black Isle (North to South Kessock), the service was replaced by a bridge in 1982. (A.M. Young)

Working the Corran - Ardgour ferry with the *Rosehaugh* is the *Maid of Glencoul*. She has served the link since 1984 having been replaced by a bridge at the Kylesku - Kylestrome ferry in Sutherland. (Nicholas Meads)

Caledonian MacBrayne's *Jupiter* leaving Dunoon for Gourock in 1989. (John Hendy)

The *Loch Bhrusda* operates the service between Otternish and Leverburgh. (Miles Cowsill)

The *Clansman* and *Lord of the Isles* at Oban's Railway Pier in July 1998. (Caledonian MacBrayne)

The turntable ferry was once a familiar sight in the Western Isles. There is presently just one example left in operation across the narrows between Glenelg and Kylerhea (Skye). The *Glenachulish* was built in 1969 for the Ballachulish ferry at Loch Leven but was replaced by a bridge in 1975. (Nicholas Meads)

Arriving at the rail head at the Kyle of Lochalsh, CalMac's *Lochmor* was built for the passenger link with the Small Isles (Eigg, Muck, Rum and Canna) with weekly summer cruises through the Sound of Sleat to Kyle, The latter were discontinued after 1997. (A.M. Young)

The sister ships *Loch Dunvegan* and *Loch Fyne* were introduced on the Kyle of Lochalsh - Kyleakin (Skye) link in 1991 but following the opening of the bridge in October 1995 they were both withdrawn and offered for sale. No purchasers came forward and a change of management at CalMac saw both returned to service in the autumn 1997. (Brian Maxted)

The *Loch Fyne* berthed at Kyle of Lochalsh with the grey waters of Kyle Akin beyond. Passenger accommodation is over three decks on one side of the vessel. (Brian Maxted)

The *Iona* in the Sound of Sleat during her final season on the Mallaig - Armadale (Skye) run. (Miles Cowsill)

The *Loch Buie* arriving at Fionnphort (Mull) from Iona. (Brian Maxted)

he Island class ferry *Eigg* leaving Tobermory (Mull) for Kilchoan in June 1997. (Miles Cowsill)

he *Isle of Cumbrae* loading at Fishnish (Mull) for Lochaline in June 1997. (Miles Cowsill)

This view, from the other side of the *Loch Dunvegan*, illustrates the unusual position of the wheelhouse in relation to the funnel. (Brian Maxted)

The last of the Island class was the *Raasay* of 1976. The vessel has spent nearly all of her career operating to the island whose name she bears from the Skye base of Sconser. She she replaced by the larger *Loch Striven* in 199? after which she became the spare vessel. (Brian Maxted)

The *Loch Striven* was used mainly at Largs until her transfer northwards to work the summer Sconser (Skye) - Raasay service. (Lawrence Macduff)

The *Hebridean Isles* operates from her base at Uig (Skye) to Tarbert (Harris) and Lochmaddy (North Uist). Built at Selby in 1985, she did not enter service on her intended route until the following May after the roll-on facilities had been built at her piers of call. (Miles Cowsill)

The Loch class ferry *Loch Linnhe* leaving Cumbrae Slip for Largs. (Brian Maxted)

The *Pioneer* makes a splendid sight off Ashton in 1992. (Lawrence Macduff)

Shetland Islands Council's *Leirna* at her Lerwick terminal. (Miles Cowsill)

Comhairle Nan Eilean Siar is the Gaelic name of the former Western Isles Council. One of their two vehicle ferries is the *Eilean Bhearnaraigh* which is used on the five minute link between Otternish (North Uist) and the island of Berneray. It is run in conjunction with Caledonian MacBrayne's Otternish - Leverburgh (Harris) service but will soon be replaced by a causeway. (Lawrence Macduff)

The other ferry to carry the distinctive pale blue livery of Comhairle Nan Eilean Siar is the *Eilean Na H-Oige* which is used on the Ludaig (South Uist) to Eriskay service. She was built at Stornoway in 1980. (Lawrence Macduff)

hroughout the years a number of ferry services have been replaced by bridges and in December 1997 the link etween Scalpay and Kyles Scalpay also succumbed. Here is the Island class vessel *Canna* arriving at Kyles in e previous year. This vessel was transferred to the Ballycastle (Antrim) - Rathlin Island route in 1997. ₋awrence Macduff)

he cruise ship *Hebridean Princess* alongside at Tarbert Pier (Harris). Built as one of a trio of ships for 1acBrayne's Western Isles car ferry services, the *Columba* was placed on the Oban - Craignure (Mull) link in ily 1964. Sold out of service in 1988 she was purchased by Hebridean Island Cruises and converted to her resent role. (R. Stewart Cameron)

Caledonian MacBrayne's 'pot of gold' seems to be on board the *Loch Dunvegan* at Lochaline in February 1998. (A.M. Young)

The ABC car ferry *Bute* arriving at Craignure (Mull) from Oban during her 1973 season on the route. (John Hendy)

Berthed bow-in at Lochmaddy (North Uist), the *Lord of the Isles* is an unusual visitor. During December 1997 she was required to assist during an emergency. (Iain McPherson)

The *Loch Bhrusda* leaving Leverburgh (Harris) for Otternish (North Uist) on an afternoon sailing during August 1997. The ship was built to inaugurate this new crossing of the Sound of Harris in 1996. (Nicholas Meads)

Passengers boarding the *Loch Bhrusda* at Leverburgh do so across the exposed slipway and via the vehicle deck. As with most of the smaller ferries, both access and accommodation are basic. (R. Stewart Cameron)

Caledonian MacBrayne purchased the *Suilven* from Norwegian operators, who planned to operate the vessel across the Oslofjord, in 1974 and placed her on the Ullapool - Stornoway (Lewis) link. She served with distinction until replaced by the *Isle of Lewis* in 1995 after which she was purchased by a New Zealand company for further work across the Cook Strait. The vessel is seen arriving at Ullapool in August 1991. (Iain McPherson)

Maintaining the 2 hour 40 minute crossing of the Minch is the *Isle of Lewis* which entered service on the Ullapool - Stornoway (Lewis) link in 1995. With capacity for 680 passengers and 123 cars she, in turn, became the company's largest ship replacing the smaller *Suilven*. (Lawrence Macduff)

P&O Scottish Ferries' *St. Ola* was built as the Swedish ferry *Svea Scarlett* in 1971 and entered service on the Pentland Firth link between Stromness (Orkney) and Scrabster in March 1992. She is the fourth vessel to carry his name. (David Parsons)

Built at Campbeltown in 1991 the *Thorsvoe* took up the South Isles service linking Houton (Mainland) with Lyness (Hoy), Flotta and Longhope (South Walls). Her large superstructure has not made her the easiest vessel to handle and she was replaced in 1994. She is now in reserve. (A.M. Young)

The *Hoy Head* replaced the *Thorsvoe* in the Orkney Ferries' fleet. The Bideford-built vessel has capacity for 125 passengers and 18 cars - both larger than the vessel she replaced although her tonnage is smaller. (A.M. Young)

The *Graemsay* entered service in 1996 and operates from Stromness (Mainland) to Moaness (Hoy) and Graemsay offering a passenger and cargo service. Although she has capacity for 73 passengers and 1 car, a vehicle is not normally carried. (A.M. Young)

Orkney Ferries' *Shapinsay* was built at Hull during 1989 for the Kirkwall (Mainland) to Shapinsay service. (A.M. Young)

Built in Bristol in 1987 the *Eynhallow* works the ferry service between Tingwall (Mainland) and the islands of Rousay, Egilsay and Wyre. Such was her success that in 1991 she was lengthened by 5 metres to increase her capacity to 95 passengers and 8 cars. (A.M. Young)

Orkney Ferries' *Varagen* was built for the ill-fated Gill's Bay (Caithness) to Burwick (South Ronaldsay) link of the earlier named Orkney Ferries. The vessel was acquired in 1991 and complements the services operated by the purpose-built sisters *Earl Thorfinn* and *Earl Sigurd*. (A.M. Young)

The *Earl Sigurd* (above) was built on the Mersey and with her sister *Earl Thorfinn* (below), they entered service during 1990 commencing roll on - roll off operations to the North Isles between Kirkwall (Mainland) and Eday, Papa Westray, Sanday, Stronsay, Westray and North Ronaldsay. (both A.M. Young)

P&O Scottish Ferries operate the freight vessel *St. Rognvald* on their link between Aberdeen, Orkney and Lerwick (Shetland). Built in Germany in 1970, the vessel served in the Mediterranean before being purchased by P&O for her present service in 1990. (Lawrence Macduff)

The Aberdeen - Lerwick (Shetland) ferry is the *St. Clair* which was built in 1971 for service between Denmark and Germany. She was later sold to Yugoslavia before being taken on charter and then purchased by Brittany Ferries, for whom she operated as the *Tregastel,* until sold to P&O in 1991. She entered service in March 1992. (Miles Cowsill)

The Shetland Islands Council (SIC) operate the 1993-built *Leirna* on their 5 minute commuter service linking Lerwick (Mainland) and Maryfield (Bressay). She has capacity for 100 passengers and 20 cars. (Lawrence Macduff)

The *Hendra* entered service for the SIC in 1982 and is the principal vessel on the Laxo (Mainland) - Symbister (Whalsay) crossing. (Lawrence Macduff)

The second vessel on the Laxo - Symbister route is the elderly former Norwegian vessel *Kjella*. She was built in 1957 and was acquired by the SIC in 1980. (Lawrence Macduff)

The *Bigga* works the crossing linking Toft (Mainland) and Ulsta (Yell). She entered service in 1991 and is seen here arriving at Ulsta. (Lawrence Macduff)

Operating partner on the Toft - Ulsta route is the *Geira* which entered service in 1988. (Lawrence Macduff)

Entering service in 1985 came the *Fivla* which maintains the northern link across the Bluemull Sound connecting Gutcher (Yell) and Belmont (Unst). The Troon-built vessel has capacity for 95 passengers and 15 cars. (Lawrence Macduff)

The *Filla* is a much smaller unit of the SIC fleet. She was built in Norway in 1983 for service from Lerwick (Mainland) to the 70 strong community in the Skerries - a 25 mile, 3 hour crossing operated twice a week (Lawrence Macduff)

The *Thora* is one of Shetland's first generation ferries and originally on the Toft - Ulsta link. She is presently used as a spare vessel having capacity for 93 passengers and 10 cars. (Miles Cowsill)

First and second generation ferries *Fivla* (left) and *Grima* off service at Lerwick. The Maryfield slipway is on the extreme right of this view. (Miles Cowsill)

The *Fylga* is also one of the first five of the SIC's first generation ferries built between 1973 - 75. Constructed for the Laxo - Symbister link, she is now in reserve. (Miles Cowsill)

One of the smallest ferries in service around the coast of Scotland is the *Cromarty Rose* which carries two cars across the Cromarty Firth between Cromarty (Black Isle) and Nigg (Easter Ross). (A.M. Young)

After her own withdrawal from service the *Caledonia* spent most of 1989 in Dundee Harbour after plans to convert her for use in a static role at the Glasgow Garden Festival had fallen through. She is seen in a partly painted condition before departing for Naples as the *Heidi*. Captain R.F. Scott's *Discovery* is seen in the foreground in her original location before Discovery Point Dock was opened. (Iain R. Murray)

he *B.L. Nairn* of 1929 was one of the Dundee Harbour Commissioners' Tay ferry boats. She is seen at her Fife ·rminal in April 1961, seven years before the road bridge was opened across the Tay. (A.M. Young)

he cruise vessel *Balmoral* spent two years in Dundee, originally as a floating bar until the venture failed and ιe was later rescued by supporters of the paddle steamer *Waverley*. The dock in which the *Balmoral* is moored ; now sealed off and is the home of Captain Scott's *Discovery*. The slipway on the left is the former Dundee ase of the 'Fifie' ferries before the road bridge was opened in 1968. This picture dates from October 1984. ain R. Murray)

Company and Route Information

Argyll & Bute Council

Kilbowie House, Gallanach Road, Oban, PA34 4PF.
Tel: 01631 562125

Route	Time	Usual vessel
Seil - Luing	5 minutes	Belnahua
Port Askaig (Islay) - Feolin (Jura)	5 minutes	Eilean Dhuira

Bruce Watt Sea Cruises

Mallaig: Tel/Fax 0167 462320.

Route	Time	Vessels
Mallaig - Inverie	50 minutes	Western Isles (pass. only)
(and summer cruises to Loch Scavaig (Skye) and Rum and Canna)		

Caledonian MacBrayne

The Ferry Terminal, Gourock, Renfrewshire, PA19 1QP.
Tel: 01475 650100

Principal Summer Services 1998

Route	Time	Usual vessel
Ardrossan - Brodick (Arran)	55 minutes	Caledonian Isles
Wemyss - Bay - Rothesay (Bute)	30 minutes	) Jupiter, Juno,
Gourock - Dunoon	20 minutes	) Saturn, Pioneer
Kennacraig - Port Ellen (Islay)	2 hours 15 minutes	Isle of Arran
Kennacraig - Port Askaig (Islay)	2 hours 15 minutes	Isle of Arran
Oban - Craignure (Mull)	40 minutes	Isle of Mull
Oban - Colonsay	2 hours 10 minutes	Isle of Mull
Oban - Coll (direct)	2 hours 25 minutes	Clansman
Oban - Tiree (direct)	3 hours 30 minutes	Clansman
Oban - Lochboisdale (S. Uist)	5 hours	Clansman
Oban - Castlebay (Barra)	5 hours	Clansman
Mallaig - Armadale (Skye) *	30 minutes	Lord of the Isles
Mallaig - S. Uist*	3 hours 15 minutes	Lord of the Isles
Mallaig - Barra*	3 hours 45 minutes	Lord of the Isles
Uig (Skye) - Tarbert (Harris)	1 hour 45 minutes	Hebridean Isles
Uig (Skye) - Lochmaddy (N. Uist)	1 hour 45 minutes	Hebridean Isles
Ullapool - Stornoway (Lewis)	2 hours 40 minutes	Isle of Lewis
Largs - Cumbrae Slip	10 minutes	Loch Riddon, Loch Alainn
Colintraive - Rhubodach (Bute)	5 minutes	Isle of Cumbrae
Taylinloan - Gigha	20 minutes	Loch Ranza
Oban - Lismore	50 minutes	Bruernish
Otternish (N. Uist) - Leverburgh (Harris)	70 minutes	Loch Bhrusda
Lochaline - Fishnish (Mull)	15 minutes	Loch Fyne
Sconser (Skye) - Raasay	15 minutes	Loch Striven

Shetland Islands Council

Port Administration Building, Sella Ness, Mossbank, Shetland, ZE2 9QR.
Tel: 01806 244216

Route	Time	Usual vessels
Toft (Mainland) - Ulsta (Yell)	20 minutes	Bigga, Geira
Gutcher (Yell) - Belmont (Unst)	10 minutes	Fivla
Gutcher (Yell) - Oddsta (Fetlar)	25 minutes	Fylga
Lerwick (Mainland) - Maryfield (Bressay)	5 minutes	Leirna
Laxo (Mainland) - Symbister (Whalsay)	30 minutes	Hendra, Kjella
Lerwick (Mainland) - Out Skerries	3 hours	Filla
Vidlin (Mainland) - Out Skerries	90 minutes	Filla
Grutness (Mainland) - Fair Isle	3 hours	Good Shepherd IV
West Burrafirth (Mainland) - Papa Stour	40 minutes	Koada
Foula - Walls (Mainland)	3 hours	New Advance

Strathclyde Passenger Transport

Tel: 0141 333 3159

Route	Time	Vessels
Renfrew - Yoker	5 minutes	Renfrew Rose, Yoker Swan (pass. only)

Waverley Excursions

Waverley Terminal, Glasgow.
Tel: 0141 221 8152

Route	Usual vessels
Summer excursions from Glasgow, Ayr and Clyde resorts.	Waverley, Balmoral

Western Ferries (Clyde)

Hunter's Quay, Dunoon, PA23 8HJ.
Tel: 01369 4452

Route	Time	Usual vessels
McInroy's Point - Hunter's Quay	20 minutes	Sound of Sanda, Sound of Sleat and Sound of Scalpay. Sound of Shuna is relief vessel. Sound of Scarba is in reserve.

FIRTH OF CLYDE

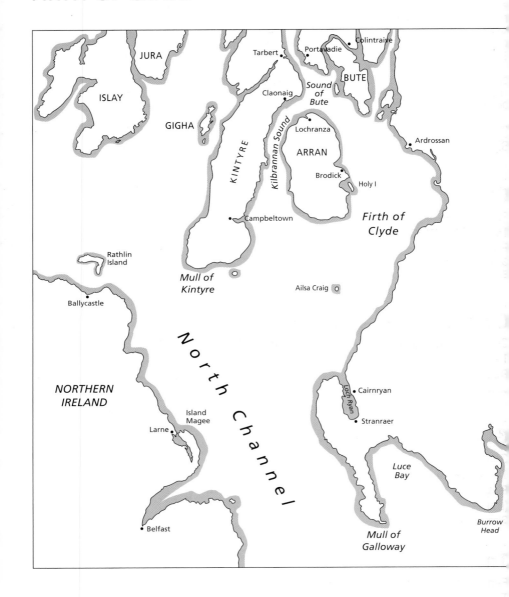

Fionnphort (Mull) - Iona	5 minutes	Loch Buie (pass. only)
Mallaig - Small Isles	7 hours round trip	Lochmor (pass. only)
Claonaig - Lochranza (Arran)*	30 minutes	Loch Tarbert
Rothesay (Bute) - Brodick (Arran)*	2 hours 10 minutes	Pioneer
Tarbert (Loch Fyne) - Portavadie*	20 minutes	Loch Linnhe
Kennacraig - Port Askaig - Colonsay - Oban*	3 hours 35 minutes	Isle of Arran
Tobermory (Mull) - Kilchoan*	35 minutes	Eigg/Raasay
Spare	–	Loch Dunvegan

Cruises are also offered during the summer (May - September) 2 times weekly from Gourock - Dunoon - Largs - Rothesay - Tighnabruaich, 3 times weekly from Rothesay - Largs - Brodick and on Sundays from Gourock - Dunoon - Rothesay - Tarbert (Loch Fyne)

(*denotes summer only service)
Ship allocation can change from season to season. 1998 deployment shown.

Clyde Marine Motoring Co.
Princes Pier, Greenock, PA16 8AW.
Tel: 01475 721281

Route	Time	Usual vessel
Gourock - Kilcreggan - Helensburgh		Kenilworth (pass. only)
Excursions		The Second Snark, Rover

Comhairle Nan Eilean Sair
Council Offices, Stornoway, Isle of Lewis, HS1 2BW.
Tel: 01851 703773

Route	Time	Usual vessel
Ludaig (S. Uist) - Eriskay	30 minutes	Eilean Na H-Oige

Glenelg - Kylerhea Ferry
Corriehallie, Inverinate, Kyle, IV40 8HD.
Tel: 01599 511302

Route	Time	Vessel
(Easter - October only)		
Glenelg - Kylerhea	10 minutes	Glenachulish

The Highland Council
Ferry Cottage, Ardgour, Fort William.
Tel: 01855 841243

Route	Time	Vessels
Corran - Ardgour	5 minutes	Maid of Glencoul, Rosehaugh

Orkney Ferries

Shore Street, Kirkwall, Orkney, KW15 1LG.
Tel: 01856 872044

Route	Time	Usual vessel(s)
North Isles Service		
Kirkwall (Mainland) - Eday	75 minutes	) Earl Thorfinn
Kirkwall - Westray	85 minutes	) Earl Sigurd
Kirkwall - Sanday	85 minutes	) Varagen
Kirkwall - Papa Westray	85 minutes	)
Kirkwall - Stronsay	95 minutes	)
Kirkwall - North Ronaldsay	150 minutes	)
Kirkwall - Shapinsay	25 minutes	Shapinsay
South Isles Service		
Houton (Mainland) - Lyness (Hoy)	35 minutes	Hoy Head
Houton - Flotta	35 minutes	Hoy Head
Houton - Graemsay	25 minutes	Hoy Head
Tingwall (Mainland) - Rousay	20 minutes	Eynhallow
Tingwall - Egilsay	30 minutes	Eynhallow
Tingwall - Wyre	20 minutes	Eynhallow
Stromness (Mainland) - Moaness (Hoy)	25 minutes	Graemsay
Spare	–	Thorsvoe

P&O Scottish Ferries

PO Box 5, Jamieson's Quay, Aberdeen, AB9 8DL.
Tel: 01224 589111

Route	Time	Usual vessel
Scrabster - Stromness (Orkney)	1 hour 45 minutes	St. Ola
Aberdeen - Lerwick (Shetland)	14 hours	St. Clair, St. Sunniva
		St. Rognvald (freight only)
Aberdeen - Stromness (Orkney)	8 hours day (14 night)	St. Sunniva
Stromness - Lerwick	8 hours	St. Sunniva

Seaboard Marine (Nigg)

Cliff House, Cadboll, Tain, Ross-shire.
Tel: 01862 871254

Route	Time	Vessel
Cromarty - Nigg	10 minutes	Cromarty Rose

SHETLAND ISLANDS

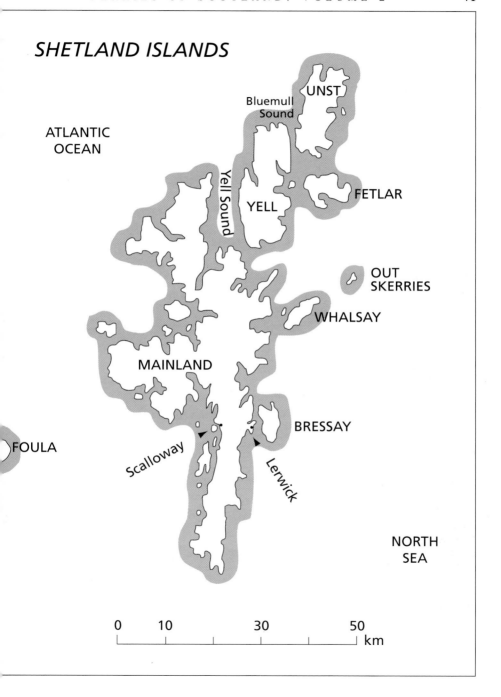

ATLANTIC
OCEAN

Bluemull
Sound

UNST

Yell Sound

YELL

FETLAR

OUT
SKERRIES

WHALSAY

MAINLAND

BRESSAY

FOULA

Scalloway

Lerwick

NORTH
SEA

```
0      10          30          50
|___|___|____|____|____|____| km
```

Clyde River Steamer Club

The **Clyde River Steamer Club** welcome aboard all shipping enthusiasts.
Throughout the year the club arranges interesting and unusual charters/ excursions.
From October to May meetings and illustrated talks are held in Strathhclyde University.
Members receive two illustrated publications per year:
1) A comprehensive Annual Review of Scottish coastal shipping and ferry movements.
2) A 36 page book, covering the history and research of Clyde and West Coast Steamers.
Also 4 newsletters detailing club activities, book and photographic sales etc.

All this for only **£12** (juniors £6)
SAE to:*Stuart Craig, Membership Secretary, 50 Earlspark Avenue, Glasgow, G43.*

The West Highland Steamer Club

Are you interested in the vessels of Caledonian MacBrayne, past and present, sailing to and from the Western Isles ? If so join over 300 like-wise minded enthusiasts.
There are monthly meetings in Glasgow during the winter with slide shows, talks presentations etc. Even if you cannot attend, the twice yearly newsletter sent to members is well worth the **£8** annual subscription.
For further information contact: *R.W. Love, 29 Cyprus Avenue, Elderslie, PA5 9NB.*

Interested in ferries?

If so our quarterly journal is compulsive reading.
European Ferry Scene is 56 pages of A4 packed full of expert reviews and articles concerning not only what's going on around the British Isles but also in the Mediterranean Scandinavia and Northern Europe. Add to that our high quality paper, unbeatable photographic reproduction and a double page, full colour, centre spread then you'll understand that **Ferry Publications** is dedicated to producing ship shape products a affordable prices.
European Ferry Scene - produced by enthusiasts, for enthusiasts.
Send £1.00 for a sample copy to:
Ferry Publications, Dept. FOS, PO Box 9, Narberth, Pembrokeshire, SA68 0YT.

Our comprehensive book list is also available on request .... don't miss the boat !

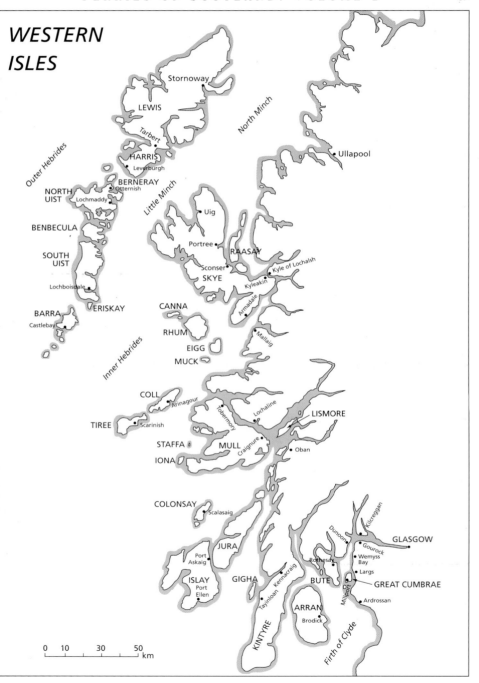

WESTERN
ISLES

Stornoway

LEWIS

North Minch

Outer Hebrides

Tarbert

HARRIS
Leverburgh

Ullapool

BERNERAY
Otternish

NORTH
UIST   Lochmaddy

Little Minch

Uig

BENBECULA

Portree

SOUTH
UIST

Sconser   RAASAY

Kyle of Lochalsh

SKYE   Kyleakin

Lochboisdale

Armadale

BARRA   ERISKAY   CANNA

Castlebay

RHUM   Mallaig

Inner Hebrides   EIGG

MUCK

COLL
Arinagour

Tobermory   Lochaline

TIREE   Scarinish   LISMORE

STAFFA   MULL
Craignure   Oban

IONA

COLONSAY
Scalasaig

Kilcreggan

Dunoon   GLASGOW

JURA   Gourock

Port
Askaig   Rothesay   Wemyss
Bay

ISLAY   GIGHA   Largs
Port
Ellen   BUTE   GREAT CUMBRAE

Kennacraig   Ardrossan

Tayinloan   ARRAN
Millport

KINTYRE   Brodick

Firth of Clyde

0   10   30   50
                km

ORKNEY ISLANDS

NORTH RONALDSAY

PAPA WESTRAY

WESTRAY

ATLANTIC OCEAN

SANDAY

ROUSAY

EGILSAY

EDAY

WYRE

STRONSAY

MAINLAND

SHAPINSAY

Kirkwall●

Stromness●
GRAEMSAY

Scapa Flow

NORTH SEA

HOY

BURRAY

FLOTTA

SOUTH WALLS

SOUTH RONALDSAY

Pentland   Firth

Scrabster●
●Thurso

Wick●

0   10   30   50
                                  km